Imagine!
Beginner

Crocodile in the House

By Paul Shipton

Illustrated by Steve Cox

Activities by Hannah Fish

Contents

OXFORD

UNIVERSITY PRESS

Hello!
My name is Rosie.
Hello!
My name is Ben.

This is Grandpa.
Hello!
Now let's read this story, Crocodile in the House.
3

'Grandpa, this is Max,' says Ben. 'He's my best friend.'

'Hello, Max,' says Grandpa.

'Let's play,' says Ben. 'Do you want to play with my toy cars?'

'No, thank you. I don't like cars,' says Max.

Max sees a horse and a lion.

'Let's play with the toy animals,' he says.

'OK,' says Ben.

'My favorite animals are crocodiles,' says Max. 'Is there a crocodile in the toy box?'

'Yes, there's a crocodile here,' says Ben.

Go to page 16 for activities.

Clunk hears Ben.

'A crocodile?' says the robot. 'Oh no!
There's a crocodile in the house!'

Go to page 17 for activities.

Clunk sees Rosie with Mom and Dad.

'Stop!' he says. 'Don't go in the house! There's a crocodile!'

There's a crocodile!

Ben and Max go to the door.

'It's OK, Clunk,' says Ben. 'It's a toy crocodile. Look. It's in my hand!'

Go to page 18 for activities.

'Mom, is my teddy bear in the car?' says Rosie.

'Yes,' says Mom.

'Oh no!' says Clunk. 'There's a bear in the car! Run!'

The robot runs.

'It's OK, Clunk,' says Rosie. 'It's
a teddy bear! It's a toy.'

But Clunk doesn't hear her.

Go to page 19 for activities.

13

Activities before you read

Talk **Look at the front cover of this book. Answer the questions and talk to a friend.**

1 What can you see?

2 How many children are there?

3 Where are they?

1 **Trace the words. Then match.**

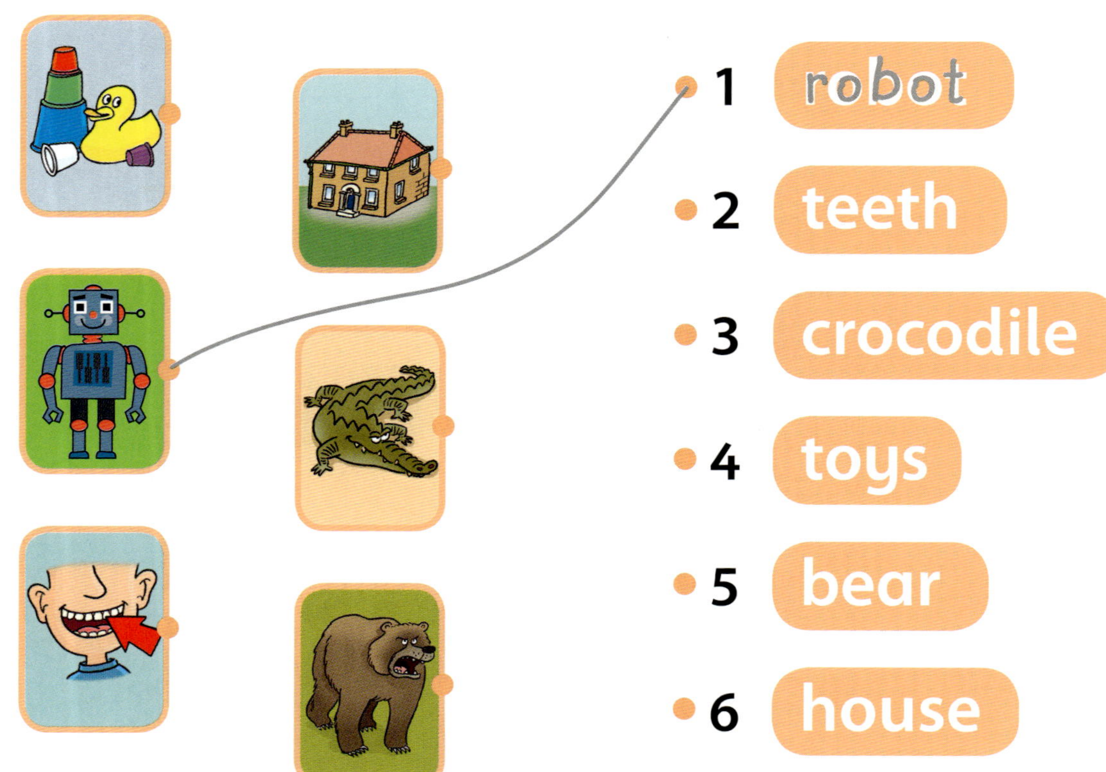

@ Activities for pages 4–5

1 Put a tick (✓) or a cross (X) in the box.

These are friends. X

These are toys. ☐

This is a car. ☐

This is Ben. ☐

2 Write *yes* or *no*.

1 Max is Ben's best friend.   _yes_

2 Ben wants to play. _____

3 Ben has toy cars. _____

4 Max likes toy cars. _____

Talk **Do you like cars? Talk to a friend.**

1 Write the words.

1 <u>lion</u>
i l o n

2 ______________
r o i d l c e c o

3 ______________
r e s o h

4 ______________
i l s a m n a

2 Trace the words. Then complete the sentences.

> **play   is   ~~sees~~   likes**

1 Max <u>sees</u> a horse and a lion.

2 They ____________ with the toy animals.

3 Max ____________ crocodiles.

4 There ____________ a crocodile in the toy box.

Talk Do you like crocodiles? Talk to a friend.

1 Match.

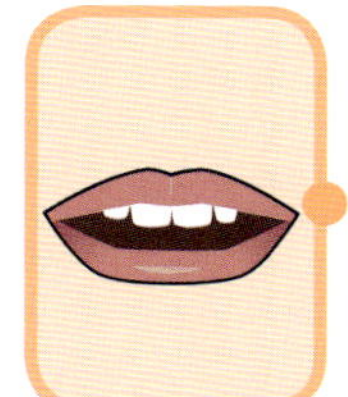

 **1** mouth

 **2** hear

 **3** door

 **4** run

2 Order the words.

1 crocodile / in the / There's / house! / a

There's a crocodile in the house!

2 big / have / mouths! / Crocodiles

____

3 have / They / teeth! / big

____

4 the door. / runs / Clunk / out

____

1 Choose and write the correct words.

Clunk sees [1] <u>Rosie</u> with Mom and Dad. 'Don't go in the [2] ___________!' he says. 'There's a [3] ___________!' Ben and Max go to the door. Ben has the toy crocodile in his [4] ___________.

crocodile

toys

~~Rosie~~

house

Max

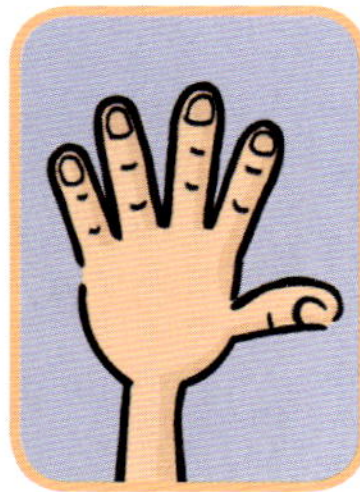

hand

 Activities for pages 12–13

1 Trace and write the words.

1   bear   bear

2   teddy bear

3   car

2 Look at the pictures on page 12. Write *yes* or *no*.

1   Rosie is in the car.

2   There's a teddy bear in the car.

3   The car is red.

4   Clunk is in the house.

Talk   **Do you like this story? Talk to a friend.**

Favorite Animals

1 Complete the chart.

~~run~~ ~~lion~~ teeth mouth crocodile
horse hand bear

Body 	Animals 
run	lion

2 Do you know more body and animal words? Write them in the chart.

3 Draw your favorite animal.

4 Now answer the questions about your animal.

What animal is it? ___________________________

Is it big or small? ___________________________

Does it have a big mouth? ___________________

Does it have big teeth? ______________________

What does it eat? ___________________________

Talk Talk to a friend about your favorite animal.

Picture Dictionary

animals

bear

car

crocodile

door

friends

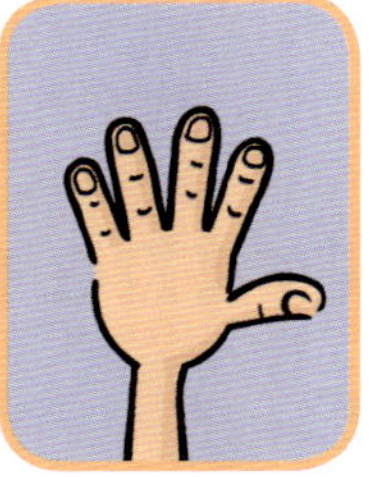
hand

hear

Hello

horse

house

lion

mouth

robot

run

teddy bear

teeth

toy box

toys

Draw and write your favorite word.

Oxford Read and Imagine

Oxford Read and Imagine graded readers are at nine levels (Early Starter, Starter, Beginner, and Levels 1 to 6) for students from age 3 or 4 and older. They offer great stories to read and enjoy.

Activities provide Cambridge Young Learners Exams preparation. See Key below.

At Levels 1 to 6, every storybook reader links to an **Oxford Read and Discover** non-fiction reader, giving students a chance to find out more about the world around them, and an opportunity for Content and Language Integrated Learning (CLIL).

For more information about **Read and Imagine**, and for Teacher's Notes, go to www.oup.com/elt/teacher/readandimagine

For a free Audio download of the story in a choice of American and British English, go to www.oup.com/elt/readandimagine

KEY  Activity supports Cambridge Young Learners Starters Exam preparation

OXFORD
UNIVERSITY PRESS

Great Clarendon Street, Oxford, OX2 6DP, United Kingdom

Oxford University Press is a department of the University of Oxford. It furthers the University's objective of excellence in research, scholarship, and education by publishing worldwide. Oxford is a registered trade mark of Oxford University Press in the UK and in certain other countries

© Oxford University Press 2014

The moral rights of the author have been asserted

First published in 2014

2018 2017 2016 2015 2014

10 9 8 7 6 5 4 3 2 1

No unauthorized photocopying

ISBN: 978 0 19 472228 5

Printed in China

This book is printed on paper from certified and well-managed sources

ACKNOWLEDGEMENTS

Main illustrations by: Steve Cox.

Additional illustrations by: Dusan Pavlic/Beehive Illustration, Alan Rowe, Mark Ruffle.